# Reading Fun

## *with*

# Little Georgie

© 2013 George T. Daniels. All rights reserved.
ISBN 978-0-9886570-1-4

Illustrated by Roy Migabon

**HOPELife**

www.hopelifemedia.com

## This Book Belongs To:

_____

## Making Reading Fun

Learning to read should be a fun experience for children. We hope you find the stories and topics in this book appealing, amusing and educational.

The Little Georgie Series will help children build vocabulary and provide an avenue to discuss a variety of topics such as music, sports, play and more. We encourage parents to join in the process of **Making Reading Fun** for our children.

# Table of Contents

# My Dad and I

# Words to learn from "My Dad and I"

The following are words that appear in this story. You will want to learn them.

| | |
|---|---|
| dad | fish |
| play | read |
| park | laugh |
| sing | dance |

# My dad and I like to fish.

My dad and I play sports.

My dad and I sing and dance.

# My dad and I play outside.

My dad and I read books.

My dad and I play at the park.

# My dad and I like to laugh.

My dad and I are best friends.

# "My Dad and I"
## Reading Questions

Where did Little Georgie and his
dad play together?

Name two things Little Georgie and
his dad liked to do together?.

# Sounds
# Animals
# Make

# Words to learn from
# "Sounds Animals Make"

The following are names of animals that appear in this story. You will want to learn them.

| | |
|---|---|
| lion | dog |
| cat | cow |
| sheep | pig |
| bird | monkey |

Little Georgie and his dad were driving to school.

Little Georgie wanted to play a game.

Dad asked Little Georgie, do you know the sounds animals make?

Little Georgie replied "Yes dad."

# What sound does the dog make?

Little Georgie said
*"woof woof."*

# What sound does the cat make?

Little Georgie said
"*meow.*"

# What sound does the cow make?

Little Georgie said
*"moo moo."*

# ...and the sheep?

# Little Georgie said
*" baaa baaa."*

# What sound does the pig make?

Little Georgie said
*"oink oink."*

# What sound does the bird make?

## Little Georgie said
## "*tweet tweet.*"

...and the monkey?

Little Georgie said
"*ooo ooo ah ah.*"

# What sound does the lion make?

Little Georgie said
"*roar.*"

Dad said "great job son."

Little Georgie smiled then said
"thanks dad, can I have a snack?"

# "Sounds Animals Make"
# Reading Questions

Where did Little Georgie and his dad play the animal sounds game?

Name your favorite animal in the story and make the sound?

# Little Georgie

## Plays Sports

# Words to learn from "Little Georgie Plays Sports"

The following are names of sports that appear in this story. You will want to learn them.

| | |
|---|---|
| baseball | football |
| soccer | basketball |
| golf | hockey |

Little Georgie and his dad were reading about sports.

# Little Georgie enjoys playing all sports.

Dad asked Little Georgie, "Which sport would he like to play?"

Little Georgie said
"All of them."

Dad replied, "All of them? Son you need to make a choice."

Little Georgie said, "Let me think about it Dad."

Little Georgie imagined
playing baseball.

He imagined playing football.

He imagined playing soccer.

He imagined playing basketball.

He imagined playing golf.

He imagined playing hockey.

Dad asked Little Georgie,
"Which sport do you choose?"

Little Georgie then smiled and
said "I choose all of them."

# "Little Georgie Plays Sports" Reading Questions

Name two sports Little Georgie wanted to play?

Which sport did Little Georgie decide to play at the end of the story?

# LITTLE GEORGIE'S
# ACTIVITY PAGES

# MATCHING GAME

Draw a line from the word to the picture.

sheep

cat

cow

pig

lion

bird

# SAME GAME

## Circle the picture that is the same as the first picture in the row

# TRACE AND WRITE THE WORDS

fish

play

bark

read

sing

# COLORING FUN

# GREAT JOB!

## This is to certify that

(first name)

_ _ _ _ _ _ _ _ _ _ _

(last name)

_ _ _ _ _ _ _ _ _ _ _

has completed
**Reading Fun with Little Georgie**

www.ingramcontent.com/pod-product-compliance
Lightning Source LLC
Chambersburg PA
CBHW041801040426
42448CB00001B/6